AWS CERTIFIED

SOLUTIONS ARCHITECT

The Ultimate Guide to Master
All the Functions and Criticalities of AWS Cloud
To Swiftly Achieve Certification.
Including 47 Functional Questions for the
SAA CO2 Exam.

DONALD TERSEY

Table of Contents

Introduction

A mazon Web Services (AWS) offers a cloud platform to a small-scale businesses like Quora, and also as to large-scale businesses like D link. Many individuals now are making use of Amazon Web Services cloud items to create applications, because the merchandise built with AWS are scalable, flexible, and reliable.

Moreover, AWS was the very first to expose the pay-as-you-go cloud computing design which scales to supply owners in computing, throughput, and storage as necessary.

Amazon Web Services was released in 2002. It was formally launched in 2006 including three services, which were Amazon S3 Cloud Storage, SQS, and EC2. The AWS platform began supplying the services which was suggested by Chris Pinkham and Benjamin Black in 2003. The founders reported that AWS can provide security features—a cost related to the developers and server maintenance—and they will not need to be worried about the location in which the data of theirs is saved. Later on in 2016 Jassy was named the CEO of the division.

Lots of individuals use Amazon Web Services. It serves 55 accessibility zones inside 18 geographic areas in one region.

Moreover, they've announced plans for 12 more availability zones and 4 more regions.

Businesses do have their personal servers exactly where they save information, but often they encounter hardships to control them. Additionally, there are actually odds that the server might crash as well as the entire work will stay in halt. As online connection is extremely fast today any firm is able to import or maybe export information rapidly and will not confront an issue utilizing cloud services. Thus, Amazon Web Services offer cloud storage so that business is able to access this time.

The cloud storage offered by Amazon Web Services is highly, secure, and safe durable. With AWS you are able to develop applications for colleagues, customers, enterprises support or even e-commerce. The apps built with AWS are scalable and sophisticated highly.

Where To Use The Knowledge And Skills You Will Learn In This Book?

Area networks (LAN) or wide area networks (WAN), companies outsourced their computer data processing to companies that had large mainframe networks. These services were mainly for items such as payroll runs and accounting services. Data was sent well in advance, as it took the data services companies weeks or so to prepare.

With the rise of personal computers and local area networks, then eventually wide area networks, companies kept all their data processing in-house. This would mean having a secure in-house local area network along with a wide area network if the business spanned regions or continents.

Local and wide area networks also mean major equipment outlays that either affected the company's capital expenses (CAPEX) or operating leases. Either way, equipment was expensive, and it had to be maintained as well as upgraded on a regular basis. The data on the equipment needs specialized backup equipment. This is to ensure data continuity in order to minimize downtime in the event of equipment failure or disaster.

As companies strive for a leaner operating environment that offers more stability and flexibility while minimizing costs, they are moving towards cloud computing. Another way to look at it is that computing has looped back around to the good old days of computer outsourcing—only on a much larger scale with more control over the systems and data. But it is not only organizations moving towards cloud computing; it is also widely used in the personal sector. People are finding cloud computing apps more convenient to use, less space-consuming, and better to back up their data. Apple has the iCloud, and Android users find using Google Drive or Dropbox easy for backing up their devices. The ever-popular Kindle uses Amazon Web Services to archive users' data.

The cloud is not only used for storing applications and data, it is also used to create programs, host websites, or run web services such as Airbnb, Netflix, or Lionsgate media services, and complete networking services for corporations.

Why Use of AWS

Automated Multi-Region Backups

AWS offers different backup methods including EBS and AMIs snapshots. Also, the decentralized nature, as well as worldwide access of AWS, makes it affordable and it is easy to store information that is critical in several geographic locations. Therefore, in case the primary production environment is taken offline as a result of a manmade or natural disaster, the backup information will not be affected. Third-party services like CloudRanger simplify the procedure, and even enable companies to immediately include backups across AWS areas without the demand for in house scripting (more on which later).

Location

Even with its fairly humble beginnings, AWS continues to grow to be the global leader of cloud computing. It today operates 44 availability zones within 16 geographic regions around the planet. Right now, there are also 14 more accessibility zones in the works, together with 5 additional regions, including China. And so, whatever the geographic preference , AWS has you covered.

Reliability and Consistency

While AWS is an incredibly helpful platform for backups as well as disaster recovery, it's likewise dependable.

Regardless of a high-profile outage earlier this season, an unbiased review found that after 2015, AWS is more effective at keeping the public cloud service of its operations than possibly Google or Microsoft. Additionally, it discovered that 40% of the platform's complete downtime during the identical period of time was linked with one outage.

Streamlined Disaster Recovery

For many businesses, including a little quantity of downtime or perhaps data loss, spells catastrophe.

For other people, the price of (limited) downtime/data loss doesn't exceed the price of keeping a multi-site/hot standby healing technique.

But whatever your business's tolerance for downtime/data damage might be, AWS's flexible platform can present you along with the appropriate resources for the disaster recovery plan.

Third-party services like CloudRanger also can simplify the AWS disaster recovery by rapidly restoring the data throughout several areas in the function of a disaster.

Simple Automated Scheduling

Another one of the many reasons to select AWS is the capability to start as well as stop different instances at fixed times. For instance, the capability to plan services like Elastic Compute Cloud (Relational Database and EC2) Service (RDS) would mean they will not need to run during off-weekends or hours. With the assistance of third-party tools like CloudRanger, there is no scripting required. That leads us to our next point.

Scalability and Flexibility

When Amazon was first founded, business engineers created a computing infrastructure that could be quickly scaled up and down to meet the requirements of a growing company easily. This incredibly adaptable method has become the hallmark of AWS, and it is among the primary reasons to select AWS. Because of Airers4you's substantial cloud-based platform, companies don't need to cope with the restrictions associated with actual computing infrastructure. They can be confident that access to servers as well as storage space can be purchased on demand.

Pay-As-You-Go Pricing

Amazon's versatile cloud computing platform enables users to automate daily activities and rapidly scale capacity up or even down, as needed. Though we have not talked about how this flexibility allows Amazon to provide a pay-as-you-go strategy which could significantly enhance your business's profits (by almost as much as 70%, as proven in several cases) and of all of the factors to select AWS, the platform's accommodating pricing structure might be the most common. This is simply because customers can end and begin instances as needed; they wind up spending for whatever they use. Also, the reality that consumers can readily correct storage/server amounts up or down implies overspending on capability as well as infrastructure, is something of the past.

Customization

However, the freedom of AWS does not stop there. The platform additionally provides a lot of customization to meet with the needs of specific businesses.

For instance, customer-defined tagging allows users to quickly monitor as well as manage resources. From cost tracking to security to automation and organization, there is basically no limit to why or how customizable AWS tags might be used.

Final Party APIs

To keep with the general freedom of the platform, AWS API would mean you can deal with the cloud-based infrastructure in various programming languages.

Additionally, it means that different third-party services, like CloudRanger, are offered to enable you to use all of the time-and-cost-saving capabilities that AWS is offering. From automated backups to RDS and EC2 instances, CloudRanger will allow you to automate common yet essential AWS tasks without the demand for script.

CHAPTER 2:

What is Cloud Computing

What Is Cloud Computing?

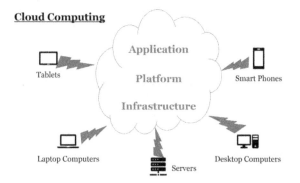

C loud computing is a way to cut down costs, secure data, always have access to your applications, and offer data storage as or when you need it. It is a data storage and acccss-sharing application/platform over the internet.

The Need for Cloud Computing

Historically, when you wanted an application, you would go and buy it off the shelf in a store. It would come in the form of a disk with an instruction manual. You would put the disk into your computer and install the program onto the computer. All data, such as pictures, spreadsheets, documents, and various files, would be stored on your computer's hard drive or some external media such as CDs, DVDs, external hard drives, SD cards, or flash drives. But there is only so much space on those devices, which ultimately means having a library full of them, depending on how much data a person has. These days, rarely anyone carries their laptop around with them since it is so much more convenient to carry a mobile device.

The Need for Personal Cloud Usage

Personal Cloud Computing

Modern-day personal devices only have so much storage space before you have to download your data to a disk. There is nothing more annoying than needing some information but having the wrong disk or forgetting it entirely.

With all the applications in use for mobile devices, a device can run out of storage space quickly. There are extra storage add-ons a person can use, such as an extra memory card. But, as with other storage devices, the sizes are limited and only one add-on per device can be used. Mobile devices can be backed up onto computers or these extra storage devices, and if looked after, they can last. But your data is not too secure and any apps you may need instant access to will have to be reinstalled. If you need access to your data fast, it is not going to happen, as the data first has to be downloaded from the storage device. A definite need for a storage facility, where data could be stored and accessed at any time, shared with others, or shared across devices, was evident. Cloud computing was the solution since users get to choose the amount of storage they needed. People only pay for the storage they use, and they can share information across the internet and between devices. Users of cloud-based storage also have access to cloud-based applications.

The Business/Organizational Need for Cloud Computing

For companies, the need for data storage grows exponentially each year. Thus, when they are installing a networking system, they need to ensure that the system will cope for at least three years, or until their next upgrade date.

IT equipment is expensive for small, medium, and large-sized organizations. It is not only the networking infrastructure that has to be kept updated but the in-office equipment as well.

In order for the staff to be able to work efficiently and effectively, their systems need to be able to keep up with the networking equipment.

It can get even more expensive when there are staff members who constantly travel and need access to the servers.

Traveling for staff members can become burdensome if they have to carry extra drives around with them or need to be near a corporate office to be able to access the company's network.

Hosted cloud platforms are the direction in which a lot of companies are moving because they can cut down the cost of a large data center. Disaster recovery is no longer a major issue, as the systems are located in the cloud, offering more resilience.

Employees have easy and secure access to the system with nothing more than a registered PC and an internet connection. Storage is bought on an as or when required basis that does not require expensive equipment purchases.

The purchase and distribution of applications are more controlled, with a more streamlined updating procedure.

The Advantages of Cloud Computing

Cloud computing offers the following advantages for both business and personal use.

Scalable

Cloud computing offers scalable solutions that do not restrict the size, capacity, or performance of the system. If more storage is required, it is allocated on the fly and the cost added to current cloud computing capacity.

Cost-Effective

Cloud computing is cost-effective in that it can considerably cut down the costs of equipment and software. For start-up companies with limited resources or budgets, cloud computing could give the company an edge over its competitors.

Moving to cloud computing will also cut down the cost of having trained personnel to monitor, maintain, and run the systems. All the technical work is done on the side of the hosting company.

High-Speed Access and Deployment

Cloud computing provides high-speed access to your system, faster system deployment time, quicker systems downloads, and instant access to software/apps without having to do a full disk or download install.

24/7 Access From Anywhere at Anytime

The system is available 24/7, 365 days a year from anywhere in the world, as long as there is a reliable internet connection. This makes remote staffing solutions or home-based staffing solutions more simplified. Most disaster recovery procedures will have at least 12 to 48 hours of downtime before recovery, unless there is a full fallback system located off-site. Off-site disaster recovery centers are very expensive, as they require a mirror setup of the company's current system. Even systems that have these fallback centers or another off-site location may suffer data loss due to the timing of the disaster and method of data synchronization. On the other hand, when the whole system is accessed through the cloud, including shared data and applications, there is minimal chance of any data loss. The data and applications are available online from anywhere, even from a user's home, provided they have an internet connection. This makes data recovery a lot more resilient and system downtime minimal.

Systems Independence

Having a cloud-based system means that an organization is not tied down to one particular location. Moving to another location is not as costly because there are minimal systems to be moved, and there does not have to be a dedicated server or data center room. Since any device that conforms to the minimum system specifications can connect to the system, costly workstations with significantly large hard drives are no longer necessary. With the cloud acting as the network platform, as long the device is compatible with the software, data can be accessed even from an authorized smart device.

Advanced Security Features

As it is their business and the need to protect not only their system but also those of their clients, cloud hosting facilities have advanced security systems to ensure that data stays safe and secure.

Cloud Platform Models

There are four types of cloud deployment models and three types of cloud computing services. This section explains each cloud deployment method and cloud computing service.

Deployment

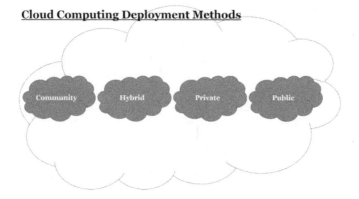

Choosing a deployment model is one of the first cloud computing decisions to be made. There are a few different deployment model types, but the four main ones are the most widely used ones.

A deployment model is the cloud-based environment of the customer's choice. This environment includes configuration, storage, proprietorship, costs, resources, and company needs.

Think of the deployment method as choosing a data center to outsource the companies IT networking solutions. Once a deployment method has been chosen, it makes the rest of the decisions that much easier to make.

Community Cloud

The community cloud offers similar features as that of the private cloud mixed with a few public cloud features. Yet the community cloud infrastructure is not shared with the public, but rather with several organizations that are either a subsidiary of the other, or have common goals and are known to each other.

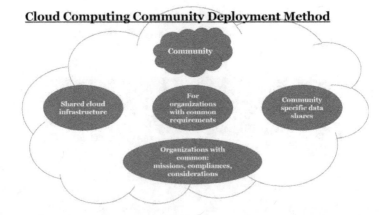

Each organization is responsible for its own infrastructure. They will have shared resources such as software and common shared data or various mission statements, policies, etc.

The community cloud is ideal for organizations that have common interests or concerns. Examples include religious organizations, medical organizations, various scientific research centers, farming communities, and so on.

Each organization may have its own private data access, shared applications, policies, legal requirements, and shared data. This cuts down on costs, administration, and duplication of work, ensuring that any common compliances, policies, etc. are adhered to and are correct.

Hybrid Cloud

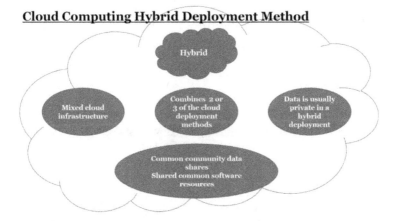

Cloud Computing Hybrid Deployment Method

The hybrid cloud is made up of two or more of the deployment cloud methods. This method is the most flexible out of all the methods, as it offers an organization the ability to share public resources, share community resources with a selected group, and still keep their sensitive data or any proprietary software private.

Private Cloud

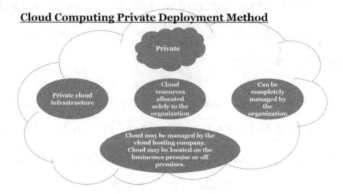

The private cloud is for the sole use of one organization. All resources, shared data, and sensitive data are accessible only by the organization that controls the private cloud. It is not the most cost-efficient solution, but it offers the greatest security, reliability, and stability out of all the deployment models.

Public Cloud

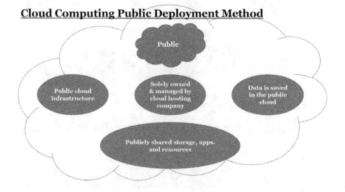

This is the deployment method that is most widely used and is broadly considered as "the cloud." It is used by both individuals and businesses who are in need of shared resources. It is the most cost-effective of all the cloud deployment methods and requires the least security.

The services that are used can be pay-per-use, but the cloud is managed by the third-party company that owns the cloud.

Applications

Cloud computing offers three different types of services, each offering a company or end-user different components. The service required will depend on the consumer's needs, whether they are a business or an end-user.

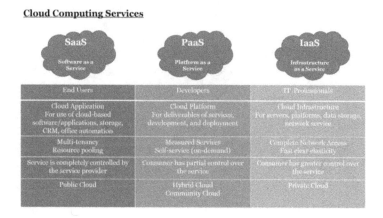

Software as a Service

This is the most popular service model for cloud computing, used by both end-users and businesses. The service is managed completely by the cloud service provider. The cloud service provider hosts a number of applications, which are made available to end-users or businesses that are signed up for the SaaS model.

SaaS is the public transport of the services. It is convenient, cost-effective, and you get where you want to go. But you are limited to their routes, time frame, and service providers. Public transport is used by thousands of others, all taking the same public transport as you do. Still, you get to choose which transportation you use (scaled to the costs that suit your pocket) and the routes you want to use.

SaaS is also the easiest out of all the service models to use and comes with pay-per-use options, which makes it attractive for the personal-use sector or smaller businesses.

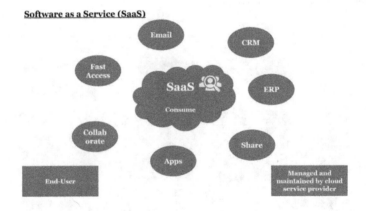

Platform as a Service (PaaS)

Platform as a Service (PaaS) is mostly used by developers that design applications. It is also used for various companies that offer services.

PaaS is like using a regular taxi service company. You have control over which car you would like to suit your transport needs. You have control over your destination, and even on your route.

Although you don't share the taxi at the same time as others, it is still a shared resource.

The operating system, storage, networking, virtualization, runtime, and middleware are all offered as a service. These services are managed with pooled resources which the consumer/business has no control over. They are offered as a service by the service provider, so any changes or additions will be controlled by the service provider.

Data and applications are managed by the consumer or business, which means they have complete control over them. PaaS offers the consumer or business partial control over the hosted services.

Platform as a Service (PaaS)

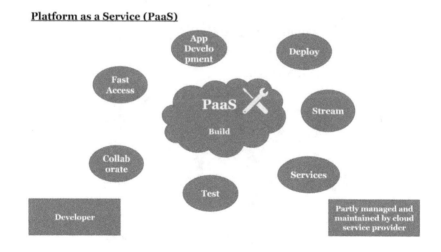

Infrastructure as a Service (IaaS)

IaaS offers infrastructure as a service and is for companies or organizations that need a more secure environment for their data. Organizations that choose IaaS have complete autonomy over the software, operating system, storage, and so on. Some large-scale organizations may even choose to host their own cloud-based solutions.

IaaS is more like a long-term lease or rental car. The business may not own the car outright, but they have almost full control over it. An added benefit is that there are minimal to no maintenance costs on the 'car,' as that is done by the lease or rental agency. Plus the 'car' can go just about anywhere without restricted routes or having to conform to public or taxi transport rules. Your space is completely your own and not shared by the public or other businesses.

IaaS offers the consumer or business significantly more control over the hosted services than SaaS and PaaS.

Infrastructure as a Service (IaaS)

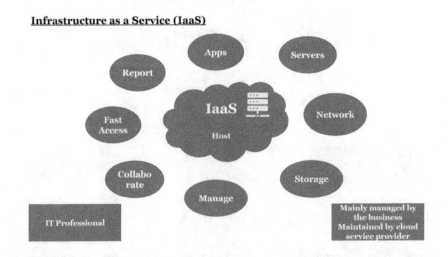

Talk about what Cloud Computing is, the basics of server visualization.

Characteristics

Broad community access: Capabilities can be found with the network and can be accessed via regular mechanisms that promote usage by heterogeneous thin or maybe heavy customer platforms (e.g., tablets, mobile phones, workstations, and laptops).

Resource pooling: The provider's computing methods arc pooled to deliver numerous customers with a multi-tenant design, with various physical as well as virtual resources dynamically assigned and reassigned based on customer demand. There's a feeling of location independence in which the customer generally has no knowledge or control over the actual location of the provided energy, but might be ready to specify location at a greater degree of abstraction (e.g., nation, datacenter or state). Instances of materials include storage, network bandwidth, memory, and processing.

Fast elasticity: Capabilities might be elastically provisioned as well as released in a number of instances instantly, to scale outward as well as inward quickly. For the customer, the skills offered for provisioning usually seem to be limitless and can be appropriated in any amount anytime.

Measured service: Cloud methods automatically manage and enhance source usage by leveraging a metering capability in some amount of abstraction, acceptable on the service type (e.g., processing, storage, bandwidth along with energetic user accounts).

Resource usage could be monitored, controlled as well as reported, offering transparency for the provider as well as the consumer.

Cloud platform models and talk about the characteristics of the Cloud and their application.

CHAPTER 3:

Getting Started With AWS

A WS has a huge menu of offered services that are divided into different sections for the convenience of its customers.

These can be found in the **Products** section which can be accessed from the main page of the website.

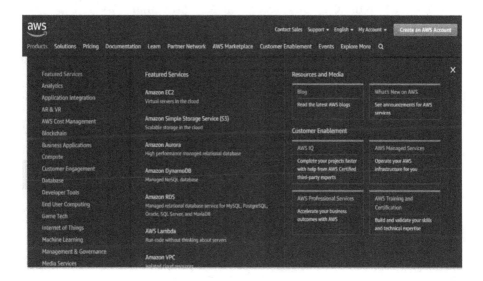

AWS has a massive infrastructure that spans the globe.

You can see where their data centers are located by going to the **Global Infrastructure** page.

The orange dots on the page represent new upcoming regions, while the blue dots are current regions. This map is very useful in finding the best region and zone for your business. If you click on the blue dots, they will tell you the region and how many available zones there are in the region.

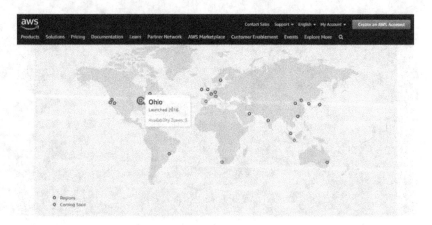

Where to Start?

Don't let the impressive array of services offered by AWS confuse you. AWS may look or seem extremely complicated, but the fact of the matter is, AWS also offers really great tutorials and assistance.

If you get stuck anywhere on the site, simply look for the **Help** button. If you are really stuck, get in contact with their friendly and efficient help desk; they will be more than willing to help you navigate through the startup process, if need be.

Planning

The first step in the AWS journey is to scope out exactly what the cloud-based system requirements are. Once you know the basics needs, the scope of the system, and what the system is being used for, you need to figure out the best deployment methods, the best service platform (IaaS, SaaS, PaaS), and the hosted services offered by AWS that may be required. AWS offers a great support service and design team that can help with selecting the best solutions for the organization's needs.

The AWS Screen

The AWS screen is quite a straightforward one. You can browse through the services and various menu options listed on the site without having to register or login to the site.

Choosing the Correct Package or Service

AWS has an option to help with choosing the correct packages or services. This can be done by browsing through the products. These are broken down into groups pertaining to function. For instance, the **Analytics** menu has a list of all the analytical services offered by AWS. Each of these services has a more in-depth overview to help the customer better understand their use.

They also have a **Featured Services** menu which lists their most popular services. Another way to explore the services is to do so by going through the **Solutions** section of the AWS website. The offered services are organized by what the hosted system is being used for, by industry, or by organization type.

Once you have a feel for the products and services offered, you will be able to better formulate the requirements for your organization. The next step would be to check out the pricing which lists the various costs and has a convenient section explaining how AWS pricing structure and options work. Once the services have been activated, you will receive a notification and will be able to get started on the new cloud-based system.

What Are the Zones and Regions?

Amazon has very high-tech data centers that are located in different geographical areas. These geographical areas are the regions, and regions have a few separate locations called availability zones.

Local zones are the areas where resources can be placed to make them closer to the end-user.

How to Choose a Zone and Region

Availability Zones allow an organization to distribute resources across them so there is no one point of failure in case one of the AWS zones goes down. If a company has instances that have been distributed across multiple zones, failover processes can be built in to make sure outages in one zone can be handled by another zone.

Local Zones allow for the distribution of services to be placed in a zone that is closer to the end-user for their convenience. However, local zones are not available in every region.

To check if there is a local zone in the required area you need to check on the website under **Geographic Locations**.

Regions are where an instance of EC2 servers are hosted. Each region will be in a separate location to ensure system resilience. With isolated instances of services located in various remote regions, AWS can offer a high level of service continuity.

Although regions can be specific to where the organization is located. Regions can be selected for services to be closer to the end-user or customer. This means if the client is located in South America, they can have instances located in North America, Europe, and so on. Always check the pricing and service plans, as there are charges for the transferring of data between the regions.

Creating the Account

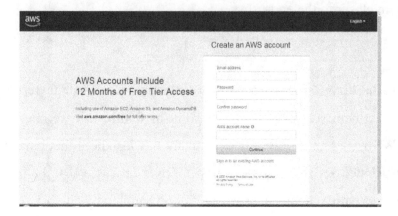

Create an account by clicking the **Sign Up** button on the top right-hand corner of the AWS web page. Enter the email address to be used for account transactions and correspondences.

Set up a password and choose the AWS account name; click **Continue** and follow the instructions that will take you through the setup, step by step.

At any time, if you are in need of assistance, AWS help and support services are available 24/7.

AWS Management Console

AWS has a management console to help users manage and navigate through their services. It is a customizable graphical user interface (GUI) that allows the end-user control over selected services. It helps the end-user run services such as applications, storage, cloud infrastructure, and any other service they run over the AWS cloud.

AWS Free Tier & Pricing

The AWS pricing screen has a lot of helpful information on it. All the cloud hosting costs are completely transparent and kept updated. Before you select services, it is advisable to go to the AWS pricing screen. There is a section there that explains the different costs and pricing for various solutions. It has a section to help an organization optimize its costs. It also has a calculator to help calculate various costs.

Free Tier

When first signing up with AWS, unless specified otherwise, the account is set to the Free Tier option. The Free Tier option has a lot of the available resources and services, but it also has set limits that if exceeded, will be billed for.

The Free Tier expires after a year, but if an organization requires more services than the set limits, these services will be charged to the customer. There are various one-time limits set on some of the services, and all other services that are exceeded get a pay-per-use rate charged. These pay-per-use charges will be the charges as explained in the AWS pricing information.

Small businesses, large enterprises, students, and organizations may all qualify to use the free tier. However, only one user account will be allowed to use the free tier account per organization. It should be noted that any services on the free tier that are used above the free tier limits are charged as a standard fee to the organization. This cost will be added to the total bill, which will include all the AWS accounts associated with an organization.

AWS offers three variations of its free tier. The first is an "always free" tier which has no expiration. The second variation is a short-term trial where end-users can test out different services and solutions. The third variation is the default 12-month free trial which an end-user gets upon signing up with AWS.

Pricing

Each service or solution may have its own cost per usage, but AWS does have three standard pricing models.

Pay-as-you-go is the model that allows more flexibility, in that you only pay for the service or resources that you need when you need them. For instance, a large project may require extra storage space for the duration of the project. This will be charged while the extra space is being used. When the project is finished and space is no longer required, the charge will be dropped as soon as space is no longer used.

Use more and pay less is a model that can help an organization cut costs for various services with a tiered pricing scheme that provides lower unit costs when you use more. This works similarly to contract pricing structures where buying a contract for two years instead of one saves you a few dollars a month. By opting for larger storage capacity with S3, you get a tiered pricing scheme where the bigger the storage capacity costs less per unit than a small capacity, though the total cost will be higher.

Reserved instances can cut costs to up to 75%. A reserved instance is when an organization invests in an upfront capacity instead of opting for the pay-as-you-go service. This would be similar to leasing equipment of a certain specification where all the configuration is of a certain capacity. This pricing scheme can be cost-saving, as the larger the upfront outlay, the larger the AWS discount.

Alternative Comparison

AWS is not the only source of cloud computing. The major players also include Google Cloud Platform (GCP) and Microsoft Azure and the Google Cloud Platform (GCP). Much is common between the three big cloud providers. We all have a global infrastructure that offers facilities for computing, networking, and storage.

An IaaS service delivering on-demand virtual machines: Amazon EC2, Azure Virtual Machines, Google Compute Engine.

Highly distributed storage and an I/O power scale-free storage systems: Amazon S3, Azure Blob storage, Google Cloud Storage.

Microsoft Azure offers the technology stack in the cloud for Microsoft, which has recently expanded to include web-centric and open source technologies. It would seem that Microsoft is making a lot of effort to catch up to Amazon's market share in cloud computing.

GCP focuses on developers seeking sophisticated distributed systems to be developed. Google combines its global infrastructure to provide scalable and tolerant services (such as Google Cloud Load Balancing). In our view, the GCP is more focused on cloud-native applications than on migrating the local-hosted applications into the cloud. There are no shortcuts to make an informed choice about which cloud provider to pick. Every case for use and project is different. The Devil is in the details. Don't forget where you're from, too. (Do you use Microsoft technology heavily? Do you have a large team of system administrators, or are you a developer-centric company?) Ultimately, in my opinion, AWS is the most mature and powerful cloud platform currently available.

CHAPTER 4:

Cloud Computing Software

AWS offers many services that are quick and easy to launch at cost-effective prices. Nearly all of AWS packages are scalable and work on an elastic compute-basis to ensure they are operating on only the amount of resources they need.

Elastic Compute Cloud

EC2 are virtual machines in the cloud on which you have the OS level control. You can run anything you desire on them. The Elastic Compute Cloud is a web service that gives a secure, resizable figure limit in the cloud. It is intended to make web-scale processing simpler for engineers.

The Amazon EC2 basic web-service interface enables you to get a design limit with insignificant grating. It furnishes you with full oversight of your computing assets and gives you a chance to run on Amazon's demonstrated computing condition. EC2 decreases the time required to acquire and boot new server instances to minutes (and these server instances are called Amazon EC2 instances), enabling you to rapidly scale limits all over as your figuring prerequisites change. EC2 changes the financial matters of figuring by enabling you to pay just for the limit that you really use. Amazon EC2 gives engineers and system service the tools to assemble disappointment of strong applications and disconnect themselves from normal failure situations.

Instance Types

EC2 gives you the monetary advantages of Amazon's scale. You pay an extremely low rate for the process limit you use. See *EC2 Instance Purchasing Options* for a progressive point-by-point description.

On-Demand Instances

With on-demand instances, you pay for computing limits continuously with no long-term commitment. You can raise or reduce your process limits depending upon the requests of your application, and just pay the predetermined hourly rate for the occurrences you use. The utilization of on-demand instances liberates you from the expenses and complexities of arranging, buying and maintaining equipment. It also changes regularly huge fixed expenses into a lot of smaller variable expenses. On-demand instances additionally evacuate the need to purchase "security net" ability to deal with occasional traffic spikes.

Reserved Instances

It gives you a noteworthy discount (up to 75%) contrasted with on-demand instance valuing. You have the adaptability to change families, working framework types, and occupancies while profiting by reserved instance, estimating when you utilize convertible reserved instances.

Spot Instances

Spot instances are accessible at up to a 90% discount contrasted with on-demand costs and let you exploit unused EC2 storage in the AWS Cloud. You can altogether decrease the expense of running your applications, develop your application's computing limit and throughput for a similar spending plan, and empower new sorts of distributed computing applications.

EC2 Auto Scaling

Amazon EC2 Auto Scaling causes you to keep up application accessibility and consequently include or expel EC2 examples as indicated by conditions you characterize.

You can utilize the fleet management of Amazon EC2 Auto Scaling to keep up the wellbeing and accessibility of your fleet.

You can additionally utilize the dynamic and prescient scaling features of Amazon EC2 Auto Scaling to include or expel EC2 instances. Dynamic scaling reacts to changing demand and prescient scaling naturally plans the correct number of EC2 dependent on a predicted request. Dynamic scaling and prescient scaling can be utilized together to scale quicker.

Elastic Container Registry

Amazon ECR (Amazon Elastic Container Registry) is a completely overseen Docker container registry that makes it simple for designers to store, oversee, and convey Docker container pictures. Amazon ECR is coordinated with Amazon ECS (Amazon Elastic Container Service), rearranging your development to the creative work process. Amazon ECR wipes out the need to work your own container archives or stress over scaling the fundamental infrastructure. The registry has your pictures in profoundly accessible and adaptable design, enabling you to convey a container for your applications. Reconciliation with AWS Identity and Access Management (IAM) gives asset level control of every vault. With Amazon ECR, there are no charges or duties. You pay just for the measure of information you store in your archives and information moved to the Internet.

Light Sail

If you don't have any knowledge related to AWS, this is for you. Light sail conveys automatically and figures out processing, storage, and systems administration abilities required to run your applications. It is intended to be the most effortless approach to dispatch and deal with a virtual private server with AWS. Light sail plans to incorporate all that you have to kick off your task, such as a virtual machine, information transfer, SSD-based storage, DNS management, and a static IP address, for a low, unsurprising cost.

Elastic Beanstalk

This allows robotized sending and provision of assets like a profoundly versatile creation site.

AWS Elastic Beanstalk is a simple to-utilize administration for conveying and scaling web applications and services created with Java, PHP, .NET, Node.js, Python, Go, Ruby, and Docker on recognizable servers; for example, Apache, Nginx, Passenger, and Internet Information Services (IIS). You can basically upload your code, and AWS Elastic Beanstalk handles the arrangement, from the capacity provision, load adjusting, and auto-scaling to application wellbeing monitoring. Simultaneously, you hold full command over the AWS assets powering your application and can get to the hidden resources whenever you choose.

AWS Fargate

This is the computing engine for Amazon ECS which enables running containers without managing servers or clusters. By using AWS Fargate, you never need to design, manage, and scale again clusters of VI (virtual machines) to run compartments. This expels the need to pick server types, choose when to scale your bunches or advance cluster pressing. AWS Fargate expels the requirement for you to cooperate with or consider servers or clusters. Fargate gives you a chance to concentrate on planning and building your applications as opposed to dealing with the framework that runs them.

Amazon ECS has two modes: the Fargate launch type and the EC2 launch type. With the Fargate dispatch type, you should simply bundle your application in containers, determine the CPU and memory necessities, characterize systems administration and IAM approaches, and launch the application. EC2 launch type enables you to have server-level, increasingly granular command over the framework that runs your container applications. With the help of the EC2 launch type, you can utilize Amazon ECS to deal with a cluster of servers and the timetable of containers on the servers. Amazon ECS monitors all the CPU, memory, and different assets in your group. Furthermore, it finds the best server for a compartment to run on, depending on your predetermined resource requirements. You are answerable for providing, fixing, and scaling clusters of servers. You can choose which kind of server to utilize, which applications and what number of containers to run in a cluster to advance usage, and when you should include or expel servers from a cluster. EC2 launch type provides more control of your server cluster and gives a more extensive scope of customization choices, which may be required to help some particular applications or conceivable consistency and government necessities.

AWS Outposts

AWS Outposts bring native AWS administrations, frameworks, and operating models to any server center, on-premises office, or co-location space. You can utilize similar APIs, equipment, tools, and usefulness crosswise over on-premises and the cloud to convey a genuinely steady hybrid experience. Outposts can be utilized to help workloads that need to stay on-premises because of low inactivity or nearby data processing needs. AWS Outposts come in two variations:

AWS Outposts framework is completely overseen, maintained, and upheld by AWS to convey access to the most recent AWS administrations.

The beginning is simple; you essentially sign in to the AWS Management Console to arrange your Outposts servers and browse a wide scope of compute and storage choices. You can arrange at least one server, or quarter, half, and full rack units.

VMware Cloud on AWS

VMware Cloud on AWS brings the expansive, assorted, and rich advancements of AWS benefits natively to the enterprise applications running on VMware's figure, storage, and system virtualization platforms.

This enables associations to effectively and quickly add new advancements to their applications by natively coordinating AWS framework and platform capacities; for example, AWS Lambda, Amazon S3, Elastic Load Balancing, Amazon Simple Queue Service (SQS), Amazon Dynamo DB, Amazon RDS, Amazon Kinesis, and Amazon Redshift, among numerous others.

EC2: A Quick Overview

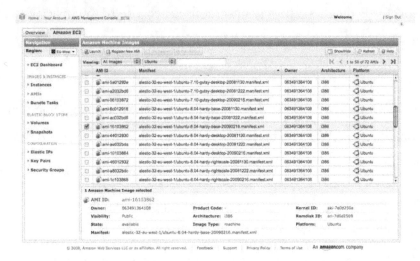

EC2 is the AWS elastic compute cloud that gives end-users a secure, highly-scalable cloud environment. It gives the customers complete control over their chosen resources and the security of operating within the AWS cloud. EC2 allows the establishment of virtual machines for different operating systems to run within the cloud. This increases a company's IT resource capacity, especially for big data and developers. Systems can be tested across multiple platforms without having to invest in expensive equipment to run virtual machines on. EC2 helps its customers overcome previous compute power limitations they may have had. The fact that the AWS EC2 environment is scalable and elastic means that if a project requires more resources than at first was allocated, it is quick and easy to get more. There is no need for the red tape of change requests or procurement requests; all it takes is re-scaling the resource to meet the current demand. If that demand is no longer required, it is simple enough to scale back down and not pay for resources that are no longer necessary. The EC2 server is easy to set up, and the process offers a step-by-step solution for the end-user to create various instances. Each instance would be an operating platform or service to be run on the EC2 server for the organization. On the EC2 dashboard, the instance can be created by choosing the **Create an Instance** option. Only one instance can be created at a time. Once the instance has been created to work on it, you simply launch the instance. It may take a few minutes for the instance to become active when first created, but once it is, you can switch to it and start using it right away. Users have a limit of twenty instances per EC2 region.

This is the default amount that is set for any account that is created. It is possible to have more than twenty instances running on one EC2 server within a region as long as Amazon has approved it and made allowances for it.

Questions

Question 1:

You are migrating to an Oracle RDS database from an on-premises database of Oracle. Which of the following best describes this migration?

a) Homogenous migration

b) Heterogeneous migration

c) Symmetric migration

d) Synchronous migration

Question 2:

The function of data consumers is to _____.

a) Input data

b) Query

c) Process

d) B and C

Question 3:

In order to facilitate the processing of real estate contracts, we are developing an application. This process requires many manual and automated steps which can take weeks to complete. Which service should we choose to use in this case?

a) Kinesis Data Streams

b) Simple Notification Service

c) Lambda

d) Simple Queue Service

e) Simple Workflow Service

Question 4:

An application is deployed using AWS Elastic Beanstalk and uses a Classic Load Balancer (CLB). A developer is performing a blue/green migration to change to an Application Load Balancer (ALB).

After deployment, the developer has noticed that customers connecting to the ALB need to re-authenticate every time they connect. Normally they would only authenticate once, and then be able to reconnect without re-authenticating for several hours.

How can the developer resolve this issue?

a) Enable IAM authentication on the ALBs listener

b) Add a new SSL certificate to the ALBs listener

c) Change the load balancing algorithm on the target group to "least outstanding requests"

d) Enable sticky sessions in the target group

Question 5:

If you need an EC2 instance to run a database, which storage option is the best?

a) EBS

b) RDS

c) S3

d) Glacier

Question 6:

If your EC2 instance belongs to Availability Zone A and your EBS volume belongs to Availability Zone B, then you cannot attach your EBS volume to any of the EC2 instances belonging to the Availability Zone A. Why?

Question 7:

What can you use to run a script at startup on an Amazon EC2 Linux instance?

1. User data

2. Metadata

3. AWS Batch

4. AWS Config

Question 8:

Which EC2 pricing model would you use for a short-term requirement that needs to be completed over the weekend?

a) Reserved instance

b) Spot instance

c) Dedicated instance

d) On-demand instance

Question 9:

How do you implement auto-scaling for instances in the ECS cluster?

a) This is not possible, you can only auto-scale tasks using services.

b) Using a capacity provider that is associated with an Auto-Scaling Group (ASG)

c) Using AWS Auto-Scaling for Amazon ECS

Question 10:

You have some code that you would like to run occasionally, and you need to minimize costs. The completion time is typically under 10 minutes. Which solution is cost-effective and operationally efficient?

a) Run the code on an Amazon EC2 instance

b) Run the code on an Amazon ECS task

c) Run the code using AWS Batch

d) Run the code using an AWS Lambda function

Question 11:

Which of the following listener/protocol combinations is INCORRECT?

a) Application Load Balancer TCP and HTTP/HTTPS

b) Classic Load Balancer TCP and HTTP/HTTPS

c) Network Load Balancer TCP

Question 12:

Which type of scaling is provided by Amazon EC2 Auto Scaling?

a) Vertical

b) Horizontal

Answers

Question 1 Answer: A

A homogeneous migration is when we migrate between the same databases.

Question 2 Answer: d (B and C)

There is the Kinesis Stream application that uses EC2 instances that perform processing and querying of data via multiple applications running on it. Then, it puts that process data into some persistent storage.

Question 3 Answer: E

AWS SWF is a well-suited workflow system for distributed, asynchronous processes involving lead/lag times and processes that are human-enabled.

Question 4 Answer: 4

In this case, it is likely that the clients authenticate to the back-end instance, and when they are reconnecting without sticky sessions enabled, they may be load-balanced to a different instance needed to be authenticated again.

The most obvious first step in troubleshooting this issue is to enable sticky sessions on the target group.

Correct: "Enable sticky sessions on the target group" is the correct answer.

Incorrect: "Enable IAM authentication on the ALBS listener" is incorrect as you cannot enable IAM authentication for a listener.

Incorrect: "Add a new SSL certificate to the ALBS listener" is incorrect as this is not related to authentication.

Incorrect: "Change the load balancing algorithm on the target group to 'least outstanding requests'" is incorrect, as this does not prevent the customer from being load balanced to a different instance, which is what is most likely to resolve this issue.

Question 5 Answer: A

The storage option to run the database on an EC2 instance is the same for a regular EC2 instance. The EBS is the preferred option because if your EC2 instance fails, you want to ensure that your data is saved. RDS is a managed service on which the database is running.

Question 6 Answer:

EBS volumes are specific to availability zones, meaning EBS volumes belong to a specific availability zone.

Question 7 Answer: 1

1 is correct. User data is data that is supplied by the user at the instance launch in the form of a script.

2 is incorrect. Instance metadata is data about your instance that you can use to configure or manage the running instance.

3 is incorrect. AWS Batch is used for running batch computing jobs across many instances.

4 is incorrect. AWS Config is a service that enables you to assess, audit, and evaluate the configurations of your AWS resources.

Question 8 Answer: 4

On-demand instances are ideal for short-term or unpredictable workloads. You don't get a discount, but you do have more flexibility with no commitments.

Question 9 Answer: 2

1 is incorrect. This is no longer true since a recent feature update. Watch out for updates on the exam!

2 is correct. This is a new feature that may start appearing on the SAA-C02 version of the exam.

3 is incorrect. AWS auto-scaling for amazon ECS is not something that exists.

Question 10 Answer: 4

1 is incorrect. An EC2 instance is not cost-effective for a workload that needs to run occasionally for 10 minutes only.

2 are incorrect. An ECS task is not the most operationally effective option, as you must spin the ECS task to run the code and then manage the deletion of the task.

3 is incorrect. AWS Batch is used for running batch computing jobs on many EC2 instances. it's not cost-effective or operationally effective for this use.

4 is correct. This is the most cost-effective and operationally effective option. remember that the maximum execution time is 900 seconds (15 minutes), so you are well within that timeframe here.

Question 11 Answer: 1

The ALB only supports layer 7 which is HTTP and HTTPS – not TCP.

Question 12 Answer: 2

1 is incorrect. EC2 Auto Scaling is not an example of vertical scaling.

2 is correct. EC2 Auto Scaling scales horizontally by launching or terminating EC2 instances.

CHAPTER 5:

Cloud Storage Software

To get started, you can simply request a device through the AWS console. The AWS then sends it to your site where you can certainly fill it with the data, then return it to the AWS regions that it has come from.

These devices are quite simple to provision, quite cost-effective, and also designed for temporary and secure storage of the data, which can be shipped in between your location and the AWS regions with the help of a freight carrier of your choice.

All whole Snow family is being designed to end up being quite secure and tamper-resistant while it is on the site or in the transit to the AWS. The hardware, like the software, is being cryptographically signed and the entire data stored is being automatically encrypted with the help of the 256-bit encryption keys which is being owned and supervised by the customer.

The customer can use the AWS Key Management services for generating or managing the keys. Upon job completion, devices are being wiped off through the guidelines of the NIST media sanitization.

Amazon S3

The Amazon Simple Storage Services or the Amazon S3 is an object storage service that offers organization leading data availability, scalability, performance, and security. This confirms that the customers—regardless of business volume or industry niches—can use it for storing, protecting any kind of data for the range of use cases like mobile applications, websites, or the backing up and restoring archives, IoT devices, and big data analytics. The Amazon S3 caters easily to manage features such that you can organize your data and configure the finely tuned controls for access to meet specific business and organizational requirements for compliance.

Amazon Elastic Block Store

The Amazon Elastic Block Store or the EBS is quite easy to use, good in performance for block storage service, and is designed for the use of the Amazon Elastic Compute Cloud (EC2) for transaction concentric workload throughputs at any scale. Also, a broad variety of workloads like the relational or non-relational databases, enterprise applications, big data analytics, containerized applications, media workflows, and file systems can be deployed on the Amazon EBS.

The EBS volumes are designed for very important missions (not to be leaked systems) which are replicated inside the availability zones and can be quite easily scaled to any amount of data (even petabytes). Moreover, you can use the EBS snapshots with the automated lifecycle policies for backing up the volume in the Amazon S3, while also making sure that there is geographical protection of the data and the business continuity ensured.

Amazon Elastic File System

The Amazon Elastic File System or the Amazon EFS caters the easy-to-use, highly scalable, and fully supervised elastic NFS file systems to use with AWS Cloud Services and on-premises resources. It is built for scaling on demand to petabytes without even disrupting the applications, shrinking and growing automatically as you add or wipe out the files, eliminating the requirements for provisioning and managing the capacity for accommodating the growth.

The Amazon EFS also provides the two storage classes, which are the standard and the infrequently accessed storage classes respectively also being abbreviated as the EFS IA. The EFS IA storage class can cost you around $0.025 /GB-months. The Amazon EFS transparently serves you the files from both of the storage classes in the namespaces of the common file systems.

The EFS is a service confined to a region and stores the data in a varied number of AZs to ensure very high availability and durability. The Amazon EC2 can give you access to all your file systems over the AZs, VPCs, regions; meanwhile, the servers on-premises can have access to the AWS Direct connect or the AWS VPN.

Amazon FSx for Lustre

The Amazon FSx for Lustre can provide a very high-performance file system that is being optimized for the fast processing of the workloads, like machine learning, high-performance computing, financial modeling (HPC), and electronic design automation (EDA). All of these workloads require the data to be presented to the fast and scalable file system interface, in addition to normally having the data being stored on the data store, such as Amazon S3, meant for the long term.

The operating high-performance file systems can normally require specialized expertise, overheads related to administration, needing you to provision the server for storage, and tune the complex performance parameters. Through the Amazon FSx, you can launch and run the file systems, which provide the sub-millisecond accessibility for the Lustre works natively through the Amazon S3, making it quite simple for you to manipulate the cloud data sets with the very high-performance file systems. With the Amazon FSx, you can certainly launch the highly durable and the available file systems, which can be accessed from around thousands of the compute instances with the help of the industry-standard SMB protocols. The Amazon FSx can certainly eliminate the normal overhead on administration, such as managing the Windows file servers. You are required to pay for only the resources that you are using, without any upfront cost, additional fees, or any minimum promises.

AWS Snow Family

The services family of snow caters to the numerous physical devices and the capacity points, which includes some of the built-in capabilities for computing. These services can help you physically transport the data in Exabytes both into but also out of the AWS. The snow family of the services is being owned, managed by the AWS and integrates the AWS security, monitoring, computation capabilities as well as storage management.

The challenge is that the data is the foundation for all digital projects over the cloud. The customers have confirmed that the AWS moving large volumes of the data can be tough. The dedicated 1Gbps network connection can certainly move the 1 petabytes of data in about 100 days. However, in the real world, it can take longer at a much higher cost. Migrating the data-intensive environment for analytics, moving the enterprise data centers over to the cloud, and re-invigorating the digital archives being required for the bulk data transport methods can be simple, secure, tamper-resistant and also affordable. For the workloads, like remote edge locations, data can also require the pre-processing with the computing power of the onboard devices.

AWS Storage Gateway

The AWS storage gateway is a type of cloud storage service that gives you the on-premises accessibility to virtually unlimited storage on the cloud. The customer can use the storage gateway for simplifying storage management, it reduces the cost for the key hybrid cloud storage use cases. These cover the moving tape backups to the clouds, it reduces the on-premises storage with the file shares which is cloud backed, It also caters the low latency access to the data in the AWS for all the applications on the on-premises, various use cases related to the processing, archiving or disaster recovery.

To support all these use cases, the service can cater up to three kinds of gateways: tape gateway, volume gateway file gateway and seamlessly connect the on-premises applications to the storage over the cloud, catching the data locally for the accessibility with the low latency.

You can connect your connections with the services via the virtual machines or the appliances for the hardware Gateway with the help of the standard protocols related to the storage like the SMB, NFS, or the iSCSI.

The gateway connects the AWS storage services like Amazon S3, Amazon S3 Glacier Deep Archive, Amazon S3 Glacier Amazon EBS, providing storage for the files, AWS Backup, snapshots, and the virtual tapes over the AWS.

The services cover highly optimized data transfer mechanism together with the automated network resilience, bandwidth management efficient transfer of data.

Questions

Question 1:

What do you have to configure to allow reading access to specific object keys in an S3 bucket, from users in another AWS account?

a) Bucket ACL

b) Bucket policy

c) Cross-account IAM instance role with reading access to S3 bucket

d) Bucket lifecycle policy

Question 2:

Your security team has requested that all requests on S3 objects be logged and stored for compliance reasons.

What should you do?

a) Configure a bucket policy to log all requests.

b) Configure a bucket ACL to log all requests.

c) Turn on server access logging on your bucket.

d) Turn on Cloud Trail logging.

Question 3:

What considerations should you make for a high-traffic distributed system that reads and writes objects to S3?

a) Instead of overwriting, write data to new object keys.

b) Enable versioning.

c) Overwrite existing objects with PUTS.

d) Enable S3-transfer acceleration.

Question 4:

To meet compliance requirements, all data at rest needs to be encrypted.

Which of the following Amazon S3 encryption solutions could you use?

a) Use SSL endpoints during data upload.

b) Client-side encryption using customer keys.

c) Enable encryption flag on an object once it is uploaded.

d) Enable AES encryption at the bucket level.

Question 5:

Which type of Amazon storage service uses standards-based REST web interfaces to manage objects?

a) Amazon Elastic File System (EFS)

b) Amazon Elastic Block Store (EBS)

c) Amazon Simple Storage Service (S3)

d) Amazon FSx for Windows File Server

Question 6:

Which of the following options enables users to access private files in S3 in a secure manner? (Choose three options)

a) CloudFront-origin access identity

b) CloudFront-signed URLs

c) Public S3 buckets

d) CloudFront-signed cookies

Question 7:

For storage of simple data types, which cache engine is used?

a)Redis

b)MySQL

c)No SQL

d)Memcached

Question 8:

Kinesis is not good for persistence storage. True or false?

a) True

b) False

Question 9:

Which of the following is true for the three different storage classes in S3: Standard, Standard - IA (infrequent access), and Glacier? (Choose two answers)

a) Standard class is more durable than IA or Glacier.

b) Glacier is block storage. Standard and IA are object-level storage.

c) All three storage classes are equally durable.

d) IA and Glacier both have a first byte retrieval time of several hours.

e) All three storage classes support lifecycle management for the automatic migration of objects.

Answers

Question 1 Answer: B

For cross-account permissions to other AWS accounts or users in another account, you must use a bucket policy.

Question 2.Answer: C

To track requests for access to your bucket, you can enable access logging.

Question 3 Answer: A

Writing data to new keys ensures that distributed components do not get old or stale data.

Question 4 Answer: B

Encryption cannot be enabled at the bucket level.

Question 5 Answer: 3

1 is incorrect. EFS is a file-based storage system that is accessed using the NFS protocol.

2 is incorrect. EBS is a block-based storage system for mounting volumes.

4 is incorrect. Amazon FSx for Windows File Server provides a fully-managed Microsoft filesystem that is mounted using SMB.

Question 6 Answer: A, B, and D

In the question, there are three methods that can be used to secure access to files stored in S3. Signed URLs and signed cookies are two ways to ensure that users can be authorized when they try to access files in an S3 bucket. One approach generates URLs while the other generates special cookies; but both require an application and policy to be created, to generate and manage these items.

Question 7 Answer: D

Memcached is the most commonly used cache engine to store simple data types.

Question 8 Answer: A

Kinesis is not persistence storage; it basically stores streaming data; then, the Kinesis application queries this data for analyzing. After analyzing, it stores that data in long-term storage like S3.

Question 9 Answer: C, E

All three S3 storage classes support lifecycle policies and are designed for 99.999999999% durability.

CHAPTER 6:

AWS Database Software

Database Services

AWS provides users with the largest selection of databases that have been built according to the purpose of the users for their application needs. You can choose from the 14 databases which are purpose-built that also includes key-value, relational, in-memory, ledger, time series, and graph databases.

The database service from AWS supports the models of diverse data and allows the users to build up highly scalable, use case driven and well-distributed applications.

You can pick up the best database for solving some specific or group of problems and break apart from the monolithic style of databases.

You can focus on application building for meeting the business needs with the perfect database of your choice.

Benefits of Using AWS Database Services

High-Performance Scale: You can get relational databases that are three to five times faster than the various popular database alternatives. It will provide you with a latency of sub-millisecond or microsecond. You can start small and scale the performance with the growth of your applications. You can scale the storage resources and compute the databases with minimal or no downtime.

Management: With the AWS database service, you are free from the worry of database management activities such as patching, server provisioning, configuration, setup, recovery, or backups. AWS monitors the clusters continuously for keeping up the workloads and running with auto-healing storage along with automated scaling. It allows you to focus on the higher values of your application development.

Enterprise Class: The databases served by AWS have been built for the enterprise and business-critical workloads that offer a higher percentage of reliability, availability along with high security. The databases can easily support multi-master and multi-region applications and provide complete oversight of user data with different security levels. It also comes with the feature of network isolation, which is carried on with the help of Amazon VPC and encryption at rest by using the keys created by the user.

SQL and NoSQL

The application developers need to deal with two of the most common things: RDBMS and SQL. NoSQL is the term that is used for describing the nonrelational database systems, which are highly available. It is highly scalable as well and can be optimized by the user for the highest level of performance. In place of the relational model, the NoSQL databases such as DynamoDB use various alternate models for the management of data such as document storage or key-value pairs.

Which One To Choose: SQL or NoSQL?

The applications of today come with more demands in requirements when compared to the applications of the past. For instance, an online game starts out with only a few users along with a very little amount of data. However, when the game becomes highly successful, it can very easily outstrip all the resources of the underlying system of database management. It is a very common thing for the applications based on the web to have thousands or millions of circumstantial users with terabytes of new data, which is generated every day. The NoSQL databases such as DynamoDB are better suited for managing these types of workloads. The application developers can begin with a small amount of throughput, which is being provisioned, and then gradually increase the same as the application becomes popular with time. NoSQL databases can seamlessly handle higher amounts of data along with a huge number of users.

For the purpose of defining the data, SQL databases use the structured language of the query but NoSQL stores unstructured query language, also known as UnQL. NoSQL databases come with the hierarchical style of data storage, which is not the case with SQL.

The users can easily add up new data in NoSQL without the requirement of any prior steps. But, SQL requires some changes like altering the schemas or backfilling the data for adding up new data. SQL comes with a standard interface, which is a great option for dealing with complex queries that are not possible with NoSQL as it lacks in any form of the standard interface.

Why Opt For SQL?

SQL is a great option for protecting the integrity of the databases with the help of ACID compliance. As it comes with a structured style of data, you will not be requiring any support for an integrated system for dealing with different types of data. It is a highly preferable database option for businesses due to its predefined schemas and structure.

Why Opt For NoSQL?

The NoSQL databases are gaining popularity day by day as they allow the users to store various types of data altogether. It also makes the scaling process easier by spreading across various servers. If you need to develop an application within a fixed amount of time, opting for the NoSQL database is the best option, as it will speed up the performance with the help of the rapid development phase.

Bottom line

Each and every business comes with its own set of preferences, which are based on the type of project requirements. Each of the databases comes with their specific style of functioning that you can choose according to your needs. Therefore, it is very important to specify your requirements before opting for any of the two databases for the development of your applications.

Relational Database Services (RDS) and DynamoDB

AWS database services come with a wide range of database choices that you can choose depending on your application requirement.

Relational Database Services (RDS)

Relational Database Service (RDS) was also has known as is the cloud-hosted solution from Amazon which is managed by RDBMS. With the usage of RDS, users are not required to install, configure, or manage the various relational system of databases like Microsoft SQL Server, Oracle, MariaDB, MySQL, or PostgreSQL. With RDS, you can spin any of the database instances that you choose with a minimal amount of input from your side. In simple words, the users need to make some fundamental choices including:

Which database software will they like to install for their applications?

The overall capacity of the database instances like RAM, CPU, and disk space.

The master password and username that they want for the database instances.

Schedules of backup and preference of maintenance.

Any settings of the non-default parameter of configuration.

The VPC or network and the region where the database instance is supposed to run.

Once the user chooses the required options, RDS plans an instance of the database and changes any required settings in the configuration. After all of these are done, RDS makes the database instance completely available for the user. The users will not be able to access the underlying host directly as RDS is a managed solution. This is also because of the fact that there is no form of SSH access or remote desktop at the system level of operation. AWS takes care of all the process of patching, installation, security, maintenance, snapshots, failover, etc. The users have the choice of either bringing their own licenses for the software of the database or by the database software license as a part of the overall instance cost.

With the facility of automated backup that comes with RDS, it is possible for the users to restore any instance within a period of 5 minutes at any point in time during the retention period of backup. The overall retention can date back to the maximum last 35 days. The best feature that makes RDS so popular is the ability of scaling. RDS instance can be as limited as having only 2 GB of RAM with 1 vCPU or as large as having 488 GB of RAM and 64 vCPUs. In case, any of the instances require more power, it is possible to easily upgrade the same to any high-end server without any kind of hassle.

The storage, which is in the underlying state, can be made ready to perform for a specific number of Input/Output (I/O) in a second with the provisioned IOPs. Achieving this level of scalability in any form of a traditional data center will require money and time unless it is prohibited.

DynamoDB

DynamoDB is a database service designed by Amazon, which is of the NoSQL category. It has been designed for faster processing of small amounts of data, which changes and grows dynamically. It is non-relative in nature. The main feature of DynamoDB is its unstrict table structure which consists of attributes and items. The mutability of database and faster rate of I/O is powered by the use of an SSD as the only hardware for storage.

When it comes to DynamoDB, there are no instances of hardware on which the billing and capacities depend upon. The primary value is the throughput of reading/write which is used by the database. The best part is that there is no limit on the storage of resources. The storage grows in size as the database also grows without any type of instance replication or cloud scaling. The multi-AZ feature, which you require to pay a fee with RDS, comes with the box with DynamoDB. The data is replicated automatically among 3 AZ or availability zones within a region selected by the user. DynamoDB becomes super durable due to the absence of replication of data, activities of administration, and scaling models of the final performance. However, DynamoDB cannot support the functions, which are complex in nature such as advanced transactions and queries. As the data is partitioned in DynamoDB for the durability, the re-writing process takes a lot of time in each replica after the successful writing operation in the main one. Read consistency is the ratio between the capacities of writing and reading.

The option of **Consistent Reads** gives the overall priority to the operation of reading, which forwards the data in case it is already modified but has not been replicated to the local availability zone. This option helps in speeding up the performance of reading, but the requests of reading need to be performed again for getting the updated data.

The option of **Strongly Consistent Reads** targets updating the latest data. It takes up more amount time but returns a result that reflects the successful writings which have been made right before the initialization of reading.

Use Cases

The NoSQL databases are not used for applications based on the web or for a modern cloud system. It can be used for storing the preferences of the users, streaming data, and gaming software.

Processing And Systemization Of The Data Blocks

Gaming: World changes, high-scores, statistics, the status of the player, etc.

Advertisement services: Collecting data from the customer base, creating trend-charts, etc.

Blogging and messaging: Building up the blog list entries of the author, message selections, etc.

Other cases where the processing of data is required instead of just storing the data. The data needs to be highly available instead of just being available for the transaction.

ElastiCache and RedShift

ElastiCache

The technique, which is used for storing the information, which is accessed frequently in a temporary location on the server, is known as *caching*. In this world of today, which is driven by the web, catering to the requests of the users within a fixed time is the one and only goal of websites. For delivering the requests of the users within time, speed, and performance are required. That is why the caching layer like the ElastiCache from Amazon is the tool that is used by the websites for serving the most frequently accessed and static data. With ElastiCache, you can store all the frequently accessed HTML pages, information, and images.

ElastiCache is a web service for caching from AWS. This service from AWS simplifies the task of setting up, scaling, and managing an environment of in-memory cache, which is distributed within the cloud. It comes with a highly scalable, great performing, and cost-effective solution for caching. ElastiCache is capable of removing all the complexities, which are associated with the deployment and management of a well-distributed environment of the cache. ElastiCache comes with various features that can easily enhance the reliability of various critical deployments of production along with:

- Automatic recovery and detection from the failures of the cache node.

- Automated failover of a primary cluster, which has failed, to a replica, read in the replication groups of Redis.

- Flexible placement of availability zones for the clusters and nodes.

- Integration with the various AWS services such as CloudWatch, EC2, SNS, and CloudTrail for providing a caching solution that is secure and is capable of high performance.

The ElastiCache service from Amazon provides two engines for caching, Redis and Memcached.

You can shift your already existing Redis or Memcached implementation of caching to ElastiCache without any kind of effort.

All you need to do is to just change the Redis/Memcached endpoints in the application.

ElastiCache Node

ElastiCache nodes are the smallest blocks of the architecture of ElastiCache service. The nodes are nothing but network-attached RAMs.

ElastiCache Cluster

The clusters in ElastiCache are the logical collection of nodes. If the ElastiCache cluster is having Memcached nodes, you can then have several nodes in various availability zones (AZs) for implementing high availability.

However, in the case of the Redis cluster, it is always a single node. As a user, you can have various replication groups across the availability zones. The Memcached cluster comes with various nodes of which the cached data is partitioned horizontally across each and every node.

All the nodes in a cluster are capable of 'write' and 'read.' Redis cluster comes with one node which acts as the master node. It also does not support the partitioning of data.

ElastiCache Memcached

It is a very simple model for caching. Memcached is very helpful for those who are in need of running large nodes with various threads or cores. You can also scale out or scale in various nodes according to the demand and requirement. It allows users to handle data partitioning across several shards. Memcached handles objects of cache such as a database. The nodes in the Memcached cluster come with an individual endpoint.

Elasticache Redis

Redis is suitable for supporting various complex types of data such as hashes, strings, sets, and lists. It is capable of ranking the in-memory sets of data.

You can also get persistence for the key store. It is responsible for replicating the cached data from primary to more than one read replicas just for making the applications read-intensive.

In case the primary node fails, Redis comes with the capability of automated failover. It also comes with restore and backup capabilities.

Parallel

Redshift can easily deliver queries on the datasets which range in size of gigabytes to exabytes. It uses data compression, columnar storage, and zone mapping for reducing the I/O amount required for performing the queries.

Redshift uses massively parallel processing architecture (MPP) of the data warehouse for distributing and parallelizing the operations of SQL in order to take full advantage of all the available resources.

Machine Learning

Redshift uses machine learning for delivering high throughput, irrespective of the concurrent usage or workload. It utilizes various sophisticated algorithms for predicting the run times of incoming queries and then assigns all the queries in a queue for faster processing.

Result Caching

It uses result caching for delivering sub-second time of response for the repeated queries. When a query is executed, Redshift searches the cached data to check if there is any cached result from the previous run.

Automated Provisioning

Redshift is very easy to set up and also operates easily. You can deploy new warehouse data with some simple clicks in the console of AWS and Redshift will automatically plan out the infrastructure for you. Most of the tasks of administration such as replication and backup are automated for allowing the user to focus more on the data and not in administration. You can also take control in your own hands with the help of the options provided by Redshift for making necessary adjustments for tuning the specific workloads. The new capabilities are transparently released which eliminates the requirement of scheduling and applying the patches and upgrades.

Migration and Transfer

AWS Migration Hub

This gives a solitary area to follow the advancement of application movements over various AWS & partner solutions. Utilizing Migration Hub enables you to pick the AWS and partner migration instruments that best fit your needs while giving visibility into the status of relocations over your arrangement of application. Migration Hub also gives key measurements and progress to singular applications, regardless of which tools are being utilized to move them. For instance, you may utilize AWS Database Migration Service, AWS Server Migration Service, and partner migration tools, such as ATADATA, ATAmotion, RiverMeadow Server Migration, or CloudEndure Live Migration SaaS, to relocate an application contained in databases, virtualized web servers, and exposed metal servers. Utilizing Migration Hub, you can see the migration progress of the considerable number of assets in the application. This enables you to rapidly receive updates of progress over the entirety of your migration, effectively recognize and investigate any issues, and lessen the general time and exertion spent on your migration ventures.

AWS Application Discovery Service

The Application Discovery Service enables venture clients to design migration extensions by gathering data about their on-premises server center.

Arranging server center relocations can include a large number of workloads that are frequently profoundly associated. Server utilization information and reliance mapping are significant early initial phases in the relocation procedure. The Application Discovery Service gathers and shows the configuration and conducts information from your servers to assist you to better comprehend your workloads. The gathered information is held in the encoded group in an AWS Application Discovery Service information store. You can send out this information as a CSV document, and use it to evaluate the TCO (Total Cost of Ownership) of running on AWS and to design your relocation to AWS.

Database Migration Service (DMS)

The Database migration service can be utilized to move on-site databases to Amazon Web Service. It also enables you to move from one kind of database to another; for example, from MySQL to Oracle. The Database Migration Service allows you to move databases to AWS effectively and safely. The source database remains completely operational during the relocation, limiting personal time to applications that depend on the database.

Server Migration Service (SMS)

This enables you to relocate nearby servers to AWS effectively and rapidly. The Server Migration Service provides agentless assistance that makes it simpler and quicker for you to move a large number of on-premises workloads.

SMS enables you to computerize, plan, and track steady replications of volumes of the live server, making it simpler for you to organize large-scale server migrations.

Snowball

This is a briefcase-measured apparatus that can be utilized to send terabytes of information inside and outside of AWS. Snowball utilizes secure appliances to move a lot of information into and out of AWS. It is a petabyte-scale information transfer solution.

The utilization of Snowball tends to come with the usual difficulties of enormous scale information movement including high system costs, security concern, and long move times. Moving information with Snowball is straightforward, secure, quick, and can be as meager as one-fifth at the expense of fast internet.

With Snowball, you don't have to compose any code or buy any equipment to move your information. Essentially, make a job in the AWS Management Console; then, a Snowball machine will be naturally transported to you. When it shows up, connect the device to your local network, download and run the Snowball customer to set up a connection, and afterward utilize the customer to choose the document directories that you need to move to the machine.

The customer will at that point encode and move the records to the device.

When the exchange is finished and the device is fit to be restored, the *E Ink* shipping name will naturally update, and you can follow the activity status using the Simple Notification Service (SNS), instant messages, or the support.

AWS Snowmobile

Snowmobile is an exabyte-scale information transfer administration used to move a lot of information to AWS. You can move up to 100 PB for each Snowmobile—literally, a 45-foot ruggedized transporting container, pulled by a semitrailer truck. Snowmobile makes it simple to move enormous volumes of information to the cloud, including video libraries, picture repositories, or even a total server center relocation. Moving information with Snowmobile is secure, quick, and financially savvy.

After an underlying appraisal, a Snowmobile will be shipped to your server center, and the AWS workforce will arrange it for you so it may be gotten to as a system storage target. When your Snowmobile is on-site, AWS staff will work with your group to associate a removable and fast system change from the Snowmobile to your local network. Then, you can start your information move from any number of sources inside your server center to the Snowmobile. After your information is stacked, the Snowmobile is driven back to AWS where your information is brought into S3 or Glacier.

AWS Snowmobile utilizes different layers of security intended to protect your information including devoted security workforce, GPS tracking, 24/7 video reconnaissance, alert checking, and a discretionary escort security vehicle while in travel. All information is encrypted with 256-piece encryption keys overseen through AWS KMS and intended to guarantee both security and full chain of guardianship of your information.

AWS DataSync

DataSync is an information move administration that makes it simple for you to robotize moving information between on-premises storage and S3 or Elastic File System (EFS). DataSync consequently handles a significant number of the assignments related to the information moves that can slow down relocations or weight your IT operations, including handling encryption, running your own instances, overseeing content, organizing streamlining, and information integrity approval. You can utilize DataSync to move information at speeds up to multiple times quicker than open-source tools.

DataSync utilizes an on-premises software operator to interface with your current storage or record frameworks utilizing the Network File System (NFS) convention, so you don't have to compose content or adjust your applications to work with AWS APIs. You can utilize DataSync to duplicate information over AWS Direct Connect or web connects to AWS.

The administration empowers one-time information relocations, repeating information workflow, and robotized replication for information assurance and recovery.

Beginning with DataSync is simple: deploy the DataSync operator on-premises, associate it to a file framework or capacity cluster; select EFS or S3 as your AWS storage, and start moving information. You pay just for the information you duplicate.

AWS Transfer for SFTP

Transfer for SFTP is a completely overseen administration that empowers the exchange of records straightforwardly into and out of S3 utilizing the Secure File Transfer Protocol (SFTP)— called Secure Shell (SSH) File Transfer Protocol. AWS allows you flawlessly relocate your record transfer work processes to AWS Transfer for SFTP—by incorporating existing validation frameworks and providing DNS directing with Route 53—so nothing changes for your clients and partners, or their applications.

With your information in S3, you can utilize it with AWS administrations for processing, AI, examination, and archiving. Beginning with AWS Transfer for SFTP (AWS SFTP) is simple; there is no infrastructure for purchase and arrangement.

Questions

Question 1:

Which cache engines are supported by Amazon ElastiCache? (Choose two)

a) My SQL

b) Redis

c) Couch base

d) Memcached

e) Redis

Question 2:

_____ is used for backup and restoration of data in terms of caching.

a) Membase

b) Redis

c) Memcached

d) MySQL

Question 3:

Replication and Multi-AZ is one of the best approaches for

_____.

a) Fast recovery

b) Low latency

c) Low availability

d) Increasing effect of loss

Question 4:

When do you need to distribute your data over multiple nodes that ElastiCache engine used?

a) Membase

b) Redis

c) Memcached

d) MySQL

Question 5:

Which ElastiCache engine is used for the persistence of key stores?

a) Membase

b) Redis

c) Memcached

d) MySQL

Question 6:

For storage of complex data types, like strings, which cache engine is used?

a) Redis

b) MySQL

c) No SQL

d) Memcached

Question 7:

When you need to increase or decrease your system by scaling out, adding, and deleting nodes, you can use_____.

a) Membase

b) Redis

c) Memcached

d) MySQL

Question 8:

What are the cache engines supported by Amazon ElastiCache? (Choose two)

a) My SQL

b) Redis

c) Couch base

d) Memcached

e) Redis

Question 9:

A relational database consists of key-value pairs.

a) True

b) False

Question 10:

In a single Redis Cluster, how many nodes can you add?

   a) 5

   b) 10

   c) 8

   d) 1

Question 11:

_____ is used for backup and restoration of data.

a) Membase

b) Redis

c) Memcached

d) MySQL

Answers

Question 1 Answer: B, D

An elastic cache supports two in-memory, open-source engines: Memcached and Redis.

Question 2 Answer: B

Explanation: Redis engine is used in case of back-ups and data restoration.

Question 3 Answer: A

Replication is one of the best approaches in case of the failure of a node. Through this, you can quickly recover the data. It supports high availability, separates out the 'read' and 'write' workloads. In Memcached, there is no redundancy of data while in Redis there is replication.

Question 4 Answer: C

When you need to distribute your data over multiple nodes, it is also useful in cases where you need to run large nodes with multiple cores and threads.

Question 5 Answer: B

In the case of persistence of key stores, the Redis Cache engine is used.

Question 6 Answer: A

Redis is a cache engine that is used for complex data types.

Question 7 Answer: C

When you need to increase or decrease your system by scaling out, and adding and deletion of nodes, you can use Memcached.

Question 8 Answer: B, D

An elastic cache supports two in-memory open-source engines: Memcached and Redis.

Question 9 Answer: B

Regarding the non-relational database or NoSQL database, it consists of a key-value pair.

Question 10 Answer: D

In Redis, only one node can be added to the running cluster.

Question 11 Answer: B

Explanation: Redis engine is used in case of backing up and restoring data.

CHAPTER 7:

Management Tools

Numerous companies and individuals are bound by their standards or some complex regulatory commitments and are still reluctant to place their data in a cloud for the fear of loss or theft. However, this resistance is blurring, as logical isolation has demonstrated reliability. Additionally, data encryption and different characters including access management tools have improved security inside the public cloud.

AWS Management Tools

Provisioning

AWS CloudFormation is a program that features an ordinary language that you can explain and provision all of the infrastructure materials in the cloud atmosphere. CloudFormation encourages the user in utilizing documents as well as offers surveillance securely and automatically. The moment everything is modeled, this particular document is the one source of the fact of the cloud atmosphere. Inside AWS Service the person is able to generate a group of permitted CloudFormation data. Catalog to permit the organization to entirely deploy approved and compliant information.

Monitoring and Working

Amazon CloudWatch might be a seeing service for AWS cloud energy and definitely, the apps you operate—Positive Many Meanings—on AWS. The person is able to collect as well as monitor information. They could further use it to observe log data. AWS CloudWatch conjointly offers a stream of events describing changes to the AWS resources that you will work with to respond to changes in the applications.

Managed Services

OpsWorks removes the need to work with the user's configuration control methods. It conjointly works seamlessly together with your current chef as well as Puppet equipment. OpsWorks could immediately spot, update, and backup the Cook as well as Puppet servers and keep their source too. OpsWorks is a great selection if you are a current user of Puppet or Cook.

AWS Management Tools Services

These are several solutions provided by AWS Management Tools.

AWS CloudFormation

Amazon CloudFormation encourages the user to control and provides the whole infrastructure by using programming languages. AWS CloudFormation lets you utilize an easy computer system file to model and also provides, in a secure and automatic fashion, all of the materials necessary for the application, throughout all the accounts and regions. This particular file is the one source of fact for the cloud atmosphere.

AWS Service Catalog

AWS Service Catalog will help the group to handle catalogs of its services. These solutions often are utilized on AWS. These IT services will embrace virtual machine photographs, software, servers, along with directories to complete multi-tier program architectures. AWS Service Catalog offers a center through which a person can centrally manage typically deployed IT services, see the compliance needs, and also helps to attain consistent governance.

AWS Systems Manager

AWS Systems Manager provides you with management and visibility of the infrastructure on AWS. Systems Manager offers an application whereby the person is able to check functional information from multiple AWS services. Additionally, it enables the person to automate functional things across the AWS resources. Systems Manager offers an advantage whereby the person will have the ability to cluster online resources, including Amazon EC2 instances, Amazon S3 buckets, or maybe Amazon RDS cases. This may be accomplished by the application program, reading functional details for watching and also troubleshooting, and also doing something on the teams of online resources.

AWS CloudTrail

There are numerous facilities that a user receives from AWS CloudTrail, including governance, operational auditing, compliance, and chance auditing of the AWS account. This particular event simplifies troubleshooting, resource modification chase, and security analysis.

AWS Config

AWS Config might be a program that enables you to evaluate, audit, and determine the configurations of the AWS resources. With all the assistance of Configuration, one could easily check as well as document the AWS source configurations and also allows the person to automate the evaluation of recorded configurations against ideal configurations. Config additionally offers other advantages: the person is going to be ready to discuss changes in relationships and configurations between AWS online resources; he can dive into intricate source configuration histories; he can also confirm the general compliance from the configurations per the inner pointers. This enables the user to alter compliance auditing, modification management, security analysis, and functional troubleshooting.

Security, undoubtedly, is always a major concern for organizations mulling over cloud adoption, particularly for public cloud appropriation. A public cloud specialist shares its basic hardware infrastructure with various clients. However, this condition requests plentiful isolation between logical computing assets. Simultaneously, access to public cloud storage and process assets is monitored by account login accreditations.

Cloud security at AWS is the most noteworthy. As a client, you will profit by a server center and system designed to meet the necessities of the most security-delicate associations. Security in the cloud is a lot like security in your on-premises server farms, but without the expenses of keeping up offices and equipment. In the cloud, you don't need to oversee physical servers or storage gadgets. Instead, you use software-based security instruments to ensure the flow of data into and out of your cloud resources.

Questions

Question 1:

What are the two types of methods you can use to configure the authenticator app on your mobile device?

Question 2:

In your custom VPC, you launch an 'internet-facing' public load balancer with an HTTP listener on Port 80 load, balancing HTTP traffic to a pair of web servers. You have verified that the DNS resolution of the load balancer name does indeed resolve to public IP addresses. Also, you have verified the website is accessible by browsing directly to the webserver IP addresses, and both instances are registered and are in service on the load balancer. However, users on the public internet get the 'HTTP 404: Page Not Found' error when trying to access the website hosted on the ELB. What could be the cause?

a) There are no NAT instance setups in the VPC.

b) You need to assign elastic IPS to the load balancer.

c) The load balancer was created in private subnets.

d) VPC CIDR range needs to be a public IP address range.

Question 3:

Which of the following metrics are not available in basic CloudWatch monitoring? (Choose two answers)

- Memory utilization

- Network bytes out

- CPU utilization

- Disk space utilization

- Average disk queue length

Question 4:

Auto-scaling supports which of the following strategies for scaling out of instances? (Choose 3 answers).

Predictive

Scheduled

Dynamic

Manual

Optimistic

Question 5:

What are the minimum, maximum, and default message visibility timeout values for an SQS message?

a) minimum=0, maximum=12 hours, default=30 seconds

b) minimum=30 seconds, maximum=24 hours, default=300 seconds

c) minimum=0, maximum=300 seconds, default=30 seconds

d) minimum=0, maximum=12 hours, default=60 seconds

Each queue starts with a default setting of 30 seconds for the visibility timeout.

The maximum visibility timeout for a message is 12 hours.

Answers

Question 1 Answer:

You can configure MFA either using the bar code scanning option or by directly entering the authentication key.

Question 2 Answer: C

This is a frequently seen misconfiguration. Internet-facing public load balancers should be on public subnets.

Question 3 Answer: A, D

Basic CloudWatch monitoring only collects hypervisor level metrics. It does not collect OS metrics like memory and disk usage.

Question 4 Answer: B, D

Question 5 Answer: C

CloudTrail and Config together can provide details on who made the change and what changes were made.

CHAPTER 8:

Media Services

Analytics

Athena

This enables you to run SQL questions on your S3 bucket to search files. Athena is an intuitive inquiry administration that makes it simple to examine information in S3 utilizing standard SQL. It is serverless, so there is no foundation to oversee, and you pay just for the questions that you run. Athena is out-of-the-crate and coordinated with Glue Data Catalog, enabling you to make a bound-together metadata repository over different administrations, crawl information sources to find blueprints. Populate your Catalog with new and adjusted table and parcel definitions, and keep up composition forming. You can likewise utilize Glue's completely overseen ETL capacities to change information or convert it into columnar arrangements to streamline cost and improve execution.

Elastic Map Reduce (EMR)

EMR is utilized for enormous information processing such as Hadoop, Splunk, Apache Spark, and so forth. It provides an overseen Hadoop system that makes it simple, quick, and financially savvy, to process tremendous measures of information over progressively scalable EC2 instances. You can run other well-known dispersed systems (for example, Apache Spark, HBase, Presto, and Flink in EMR), and then interface with information in different AWS information stores (for example, S3 and DynamoDB. EMR Notebooks). In light of the prevalent Jupyter Notebook, gives an improvement and coordinated effort condition for ad hoc questioning and exploratory examination. Amazon EMR safely and dependably handles a wide arrangement of enormous information use cases, including log investigation, financial analysis, data transformations (ETL), web ordering, AI, logical reenactment, and bioinformatics.

Cloud Search

Cloud Search tends to be utilized to make an internet searcher for your site. It is an overseen administration in the AWS Cloud, that makes it straightforward and financially savvy to set up, oversee, and scale a search solution for your site or application. Cloud Search underpins 34 languages and well-known inquiry features, for example, featuring, autocomplete, and geospatial search.

Elastic Search Service

Elastic Search Service is similar to Cloud Search; however, it offers more features like application observing. This service makes it simple to send, secure, work, and scale Elastic search to look at, analyze, and imagine information continuously. With Elastic Search

Service, you get simple-to-utilize APIs and ongoing examination capacities to control use-cases, for example, log investigation, application observing, full-text search, and clickstream examination, with big business grade accessibility, adaptability, and security. The administration offers combinations with open source apparatuses like Kibana and Logstash for information ingestion and perception. It additionally coordinates flawlessly with different AWS administrations, for example, Virtual Private Cloud (VPC), AWS Key Management System (AWS KMS), AWS Lambda, AWS Identity and Access Management (IAM), Kinesis Data Firehose, Cognito, and CloudWatch, with the goal that you can go from crude information to noteworthy bits of knowledge rapidly.

Amazon Kinesis Data Firehose

Kinesis Data Firehose is the most straightforward approach to dependable stack streaming information into information stores and analytics devices. It can catch, change, and load stream information into S3, Redshift, Elastic search Service, and Splunk, empowering close to ongoing analytics with existing business insight apparatuses and dashboards you're utilizing today. It is a completely overseen administration that consequently scales to coordinate the throughput of your information and requires no progressing administration. It can cluster, transform, pack, and encrypt the information before loading it, limiting the measure of storage utilized at the destination and expanding security.

Amazon Kinesis Data Analytics

Kinesis Data Analytics is the most straightforward approach to dissect streaming information, increase significant bits of knowledge, and react to your business and client needs progressively. It lessens the complexity of building, overseeing, and coordinating streaming applications with different AWS administrations. SQL clients can, undoubtedly, inquire streaming information or assemble whole streaming applications using layouts and an intuitive SQL proofreader.

Java engineers can also rapidly build complex streaming applications utilizing open source Java libraries and AWS reconciliations to change and examine information progressively.

Kinesis Data Analytics deals with everything required to run your inquiries constantly. It scales consequently to coordinate the volume and throughput pace of your approaching information.

Amazon Kinesis Data Streams

Kinesis Data Streams (KDS) is a largely adaptable and tough real-time information-spilling administration. KDS can constantly catch gigabytes of information every second from a significant number of sources, for example, site clickstreams, financial transactions, IT logs, database event streams, internet-based life nourishes, and location-tracking events.

The information gathered is accessible in milliseconds to empower ongoing examination use cases; for example, constant dashboards, continuous inconsistency identification, dynamic estimating, and more.

Quick Sight

This is a business investigation device that enables you to make representations in a rich dashboard for information in AWS. For example, S3, Dynamo DB, and so forth. Quick Sight is a fast, cloud-powered business knowledge (BI) administration that makes it simple for you to convey bits of knowledge to everybody in your association. It allows you to make and distribute interactive dashboards that can be accessed from browsers or cell phones. You can install dashboards into your applications, furnishing your clients with a ground-breaking self-administration examination. Quick Sight effectively scales to a large number of clients with no software to install, servers to convey, or a framework to oversee.

AWS Lake Formation

This is an assistance that sets up a safe information lake in a few days. An information lake is a brought together, curated, and verified archive that stores all of your information, both in its unique structure and arranged for analysis. An information lake empowers you to analyze silos and join various kinds of analytics to pick up bits of knowledge and guide better business choices.

So, setting up and overseeing information lakes today includes a great deal of manual, convoluted, and tedious tasks. This work incorporates stacking information from differing sources, checking those information streams, setting up partitions, turning on encryption and overseeing keys, and re-organizing information into a columnar configuration. It also involves characterizing transforming jobs and observing their activity; configuring access control settings; coordinating connected records; de-duplicating repetitive information; giving access to informational indexes; and auditing access after some time.

Making an information lake with Lake Formation is as straightforward as characterizing where your information resides and what information access and security policies you need to apply. Lake Formation then gathers and catalogs information from databases and item storage, moves the information into your new S3 data lake, cleans, and groups information using AI calculations. It grants safe access to your delicate information. Your clients would then be able to get to a unified list of information that depicts accessible informational collections and their appropriate utilization. At that point, your clients influence these informational indexes with their decision of analytics and AI administrations, similar to EMR for Apache Spark, Redshift, Athena, Sage Maker, and Quick Sight.

Amazon Managed Streaming for Kafka (MSK)

Managed Streaming for Kafka (MSK) is a completely overseen administration that makes it easy for you to build and run applications that use Apache Kafka to process streaming information. Apache Kafka is an open-source stage for building constant gushing information pipelines and applications. With MSK, you can utilize Apache Kafka APIs to populate information lakes, stream changes to and from databases, and power AI and analytics applications.

Apache Kafka groups are trying to arrange, scale, and oversee production. When you run Apache Kafka all alone, you have to manage servers, design Apache Kafka physically, replace servers when they come up short, coordinate server fixes and updates, engineer the cluster for high accessibility, guarantee the information is solidly stored and safe, set up observing and alerts, and cautiously plan to scale events to help load changes. Managed Streaming for Kafka makes it simple for you to assemble and run production applications on Apache Kafka without requiring Apache Kafka foundation management aptitude. That implies you invest less energy overseeing framework and additional time building applications.

With a couple of clicks in the MSK console, you can make profoundly accessible Apache Kafka groups with settings and designs dependent on Apache Kafka's sending best practices. MSK naturally monitors and runs your Apache Kafka clusters. It also constantly screens cluster wellbeing and naturally replaces unfortunate nodes with no downtime to your application. Furthermore, MSK verifies your Apache Kafka group by scrambling information in a very still way.

Questions

Question 1:

You can migrate from a VPN connection to AWS Direct Connect using _____.

a) CIDR

b) OSPF

c) RIP

d) BGP

Question 2:

Which is not part of a Cloud Adoption Framework component?

a) Creation of a strong business case for cloud adoption

b) Incentive and career management, aligned with evolving roles

c)   Identity and access management modes change

d) Align KPIs with newly enabled business capabilities

e)   Reinvent business processes to take advantage of new capabilities

Question 3:

AWS CloudFront Distribution types are _____. (Select two)

a) Horizontal

b) Web

c) RTMP

d) All of the above

Question 4:

To restrict any user belonging to a specific country from accessing the content, which feature of AWS CloudFront is used?

a) CNAME

b) Geo-restriction

c) Zone apex

d) Invalidation

Question 5:

AWS CloudFront can work with the non-origin server as well. True or false?

a) True

b) False

Question 6:

Which features of AWS CloudFront can you use to remove malicious or harmful objects before its expiration time from all edge locations?

a) CNAME

b) Zone Apex

c) Invalidation

d) Geo-restriction

Question 7:

What are the HTTP methods that are not cached in CloudFront Edge Location?

a) PUT, POST, PATCH and DELETE

b) PUT, POST, PATCH and GET

c) PUT, GET, OPTION and DELETE

d) HEAD, POST, PATCH and GET

Question 8:

Amazon Route 53 does not perform _____.

a)   Health checks

b)   Domain registration

c)   Load balancing

d)   DNS services

Question 9:

Which of the following converts a human-friendly domain into the Internet Protocol (IP) address?

a) DNS

b) CDN

c) Route 53

d) None of the above

Question 10:

You can create a VPC with the 192.168.1.0/30 netmask.

True

False

Answers

Question 1 Answer: D

You can migrate from a VPN connection to Direct Connect using BGP. Make sure that your VPN connection has a higher BGP cost.

Question 2 Answer: E

The Cloud Adoption Framework concentrates on the early stages of cloud adoption.

Any reinvention of the business process is therefore not inherently considered as a part of CAF.

Question 3 Answer: B

Amazon CloudFront has two types of distribution Web and RTMP. The limit of web distribution per account is 200, and RTMP per account is 100.

Question 4 Answer: B

Geo-restriction means you can restrict your content access in countries where you do not want to show your content.

You can blacklist all countries for which you want to restrict your content, or you can whitelist the countries for which you want to allow access to your content.

Question 5 Answer: A

Amazon CloudFront can work as an origin server or non-origin server. As an origin server, it includes Amazon EC2, Amazon S3 bucket, and Elastic Loud balancing or Route 53; and as a non-origin server, it includes on-premises web servers.

Question 6 Answer: C

Through an invalidation API, you can remove malicious or harmful objects before their expiration time from all edge locations. That is an invalidation request.

Question 7 Answer: A

CloudFront supports GET, POST, HEAD, PUT, PATCH, DELETE, and OPTIONS HTTP requests. PUT, POST, PATCH and DELETE requests, responses are not cached in CloudFront.

Question 8 Answer: D

Amazon Route 53, a DNS Web service, is scalable, highly available, and a cost-effective medium to direct the visitors to a website, a virtual server, or a load balancer.

Question 9 Answer: C

For geo-location routing, you need to be sure you have a default route in the case that the location cannot be determined.

Question 10 Answer:

False, because the allowed netmask limit for an AWS VPC is /16 to /28 CIDR range.

Conclusion

A great quarry is built on the fact that the right person is in the right place at the right time. Being the right person is all about you—your ability to work hard and develop productive working relationships, and your intelligence. These controlled carp will help you succeed regardless of the field or role in which you work.

But to get to the right place, there is much in common with the observation where there is a new market that would allow some kind of innovation and will be planted its flag. People who moved to the automotive industry in 1920, or the television industry of the 1950s or the Internet in the 1990s, faced huge opportunities because the new market required expertise that would allow construction big business.

Technological innovations create major flaws in the industry, making knowledge and experience invaluable. If you believe AWS is the next-generation platform, you could be at the right place at the right time.

Amazon Web Services provides an extensive range of worldwide cloud-based goods which include computing, storage, databases, analytics, social networking, mobile, creator tools, management tools, IT, safety measures, as well enterprise applications. They are on-demand, made in seconds, with pay-as-you-go pricing. From information warehousing to deployment equipment, web directories to content delivery, more than 140 AWS services can be found. Innovative services may be provisioned fast, without the initial capital expense; this enables businesses, startups, medium-sized and small business organizations, and clients in the public sector to use the building blocks. They have to react fast to changing company demands. This white paper gives you an introduction to the advantages of the AWS Cloud and also introduces you to the solutions which form the platform.

Thank you for downloading this book